KEEP CALM AND COLOR ON

75 STRESS-RELIEVING DESIGNS FOR TRYING TIMES

CASTLE POINT BOOKS
NEW YORK

For information, address St. Martin's Press,
120 Broadway, New York, NY 10271.

www.castlepointbooks.com

The Castle Point Books trademark is owned by Castle Point Publishing, LLC.
Castle Point books are published and distributed by St. Martin's Press.

ISBN 978-1-250-09333-2

Images used via license from Shutterstock.com

Our books may be purchased in bulk for promotional,
educational, or business use. Please contact your local
bookseller or the Macmillan Corporate and Premium Sales
Department at 1-800-221-7945, extension 5442, or by
email at MacmillanSpecialMarkets@macmillan.com.

Second Edition: 2020

10 9 8 7 6 5 4 3 2 1

summer

Happy!
me
mad!
not me

friends
family
clients
election
Post office
COVID
FUTURE